PAGEANTRY OF BRITAIN IN COLOUR

Pageantry of Britain in colour

Introduction and commentaries by
Garry Hogg

B. T. BATSFORD LTD, LONDON

Acknowledgments

The Publishers would like to thank the following for permission to
reproduce photographs appearing in this book:
British Tourist Authority for pages 17, 21, 25, 51, 55, 59, 61
Central Office of Information for pages 37 and 45
Noel Habgood for page 47
Fox Photos Ltd for pages 23, 27, 35, 53, 63
J. Allan Cash for pages 41 and 49
Feature-Pix for page 39
Press Association for page 31
Keystone Press Agency Ltd for page 33
Scottish Tourist Board for page 57
Spectrum Colour for pages 19 and 43
Thomas Photos (Oxford) for page 29

First published 1974

© B. T. Batsford 1974

Filmset by Servis Filmsetting Ltd, Manchester
Printed and bound in Great Britain by Wm. Clowes & Sons Ltd, Beccles, Suffolk
for the publishers B. T. Batsford Ltd, 4 Fitzhardinge Street, London W1H 0AH

ISBN 0 7134 2829 5

Contents

Introduction

Like generalisations and superlatives, claims to uniqueness are rightly suspect. The 'fastest', 'largest', 'oldest', 'longest', 'highest', 'deepest' and indeed 'mostest' generally in *The Guinness Book of Records* have to be revised annually, for records of so many kinds are being continually broken. As for uniqueness: in our infinitely variegated world this claim too is rarely possible to substantiate. The sponsors of the bridge erected across the southern end of the Bosporus between Istanbul and Uskudar justifiably claim that theirs is the only bridge in the world that links one continent with another; but already there is talk of a bridge to span the Bering Strait along the line of the Arctic Circle. This will link Eastern Europe with North America and Canada: a man-made structure replacing the natural bridge that in remote geological times linked the two continents by way of the Aleutian Islands. So, claims should always be made with caution.

One claim that may however be made with reasonable assurance is that no country in the world surpasses Britain in the wealth and variety of her customs and traditions. You could take the year's calendar and stick a pin into any date on it between 1st January and 31st December and find that one or more traditional events took place on that date.

Flick the pages over at random. 6th July: the Mayor of Rochester, Admiral of the Medway, 'holds court' on a decorated barge off Rochester pier to swear-in the water bailiffs and prescribe the exact period of the oyster-culling season for that year. 1st March is not only celebrated by the Welsh as St David's Day, it is the date of a ceremony known as Whuppity Scoorie, peculiar to Lanark, in the Scottish Lowlands. On 2nd August the Woodmen of Arden assemble at Meriden, the geographic heart of England, for their annual archery contest. 26th November is the date when, at Ashburton, the eleven-centuries-old ceremony of electing Portreeve, Pig Driver, Market Surveyor, Ale Taster and Bread Weigher and other officials peculiar to this small Devonshire market town is held. 3rd February is the date when two candles are placed in the form of a St Andrew's Cross on the altar of the Church of St Etheldreda, Holborn, in memory of the martyred St Blaise; sufferers from throat complaints come to kneel before the altar in the hope of being cured, as was a Croatian boy many centuries ago when St Blaise's finger touched his throat. 21st December sees the Pin and Candle Auction at Old Bolingbroke, Lincolnshire.

Half-a-dozen traditional customs, chosen at random from the many hundreds still maintained even in this age of ever-increasing sophistication. Admittedly, none of these – with the possible exception of the first – can really be termed spectacular, and so do not truly belong to the class covered by the word Pageantry. But just as it is difficult to establish an acceptable dividing-line between Custom and Tradition, so it is often difficult to draw a line between these and true Pageantry.

The element common to all dictionary definitions of this word lies in some such phrase as 'colourful spectacle', with the implication of 'movement'; the word 'procession' is often used; and 'dramatic scenes'; and 'succession of tableaux'. But always the idea of brilliance, of colour, of splendour is associated in the mind with the word Pageantry; and nowhere is this more amply illustrated than in Britain.

There is a good reason for this being so: not only are we a nation of traditionalists, we are among the very few surviving monarchies; and Royalty presupposes Pageantry. All down the centuries our successive reigning monarchs have embarked upon their Royal Progresses between palace and palace, from one magnificent baronial hall or ducal seat across the country to another, accompanied by vast retinues of courtiers and servants, quartering the land they rule to the wonderment of the ordinary folk and often to the hopeless impoverishment of their reluctant hosts.

Such Royal Progresses as these are of course no longer the order of the day. But the reigning monarch does still drive in formal state through the streets of London. One such Royal Progress is from Buckingham Palace to the Palace of Westminster, Her Majesty riding in the historic Irish State Coach escorted by her Household Cavalry, for the State Opening of Parliament. Her arrival is heralded by a 21-gun salute fired in St James's Park by the King's Troop of the Royal Horse Artillery. It is a tradition that, in essence, dates back more than 700 years.

Another Royal Progress is the one that culminates in the splendid ceremony known as Trooping the Colour. Again the Queen drives in state from Buckingham Palace with her Sovereign's Mounted Escort, but on this occasion she is bound for Horse Guards Parade, off Whitehall, where she takes the salute mounted on horseback.

Yet another Royal Progress, less colourful perhaps but certainly an occasion for a brilliant assembly of colour and high fashion among the spectators, takes place on the racecourse at Ascot which was first opened in state by Queen Anne more than two and a half centuries ago. This is 'Royal Ascot', for ever since it was instituted in 1711 it has been patronised by Royalty. The Queen arrives from Windsor Castle and, in an open carriage drawn by the traditional Windsor greys and bays, drives round the racecourse to the Royal Box; the ceremonial drive was inaugurated, however, not by Queen Anne but by George IV.

In these and other Royal Progresses the pageantry involves movement. But there are many other examples of royal pageantry in which, though the setting is regal and the occasion brilliant, this particular element plays no part. There are the Royal Investitures, for instance, ordinarily held in the early part of the year following the New Year Honours List and in the latter part of the year following the Royal Birthday Honours List. Knighthoods and baronetcies and other titles, as well as the many lesser awards, are bestowed on the recipients by Her Majesty in the Ball Room at Buckingham Palace. The most impressive of the individual awards is of course that of a knighthood, when the recipient kneels on a stool at his Sovereign's feet while she touches him lightly first on one shoulder and then on the other with a Scots Guard sword. These investitures are attended only by relatively few, for each recipient may be accompanied by only one or two members of his or her family.

Second only to Royal Pageantry is that in which the armed services – especially the army – are primarily involved. The two mingle, of course, in the ceremony of Trooping the Colour on Horse Guards Parade. It is the Guards of various regiments who provide the pageantry of the Buckingham Palace Changing of the Guard, at which the Queen is not present, and the ceremony at Edinburgh Castle known as the Military Tattoo is naturally dominated by the Scottish regiments.

The Lancashire Fusiliers, one of six regiments that inflicted a crushing defeat on the French at Minden during the Seven Years' War, celebrate this victory in a picturesque fashion. Their 'Minden Day' is 1st August and begins with the playing of the Minden March by the Drum Corps parading round the barracks, their drums decorated with red and yellow roses. The men wear one yellow and one red rose in their caps – a reminder of the occasion in 1759 when their forbears plucked roses in a garden after their victory.

There is a somewhat bizarre feature of these Minden Day celebrations: in the officers' mess all those who have joined the regiment during the past year are required to take a rose from a champagne-filled silver bowl and eat it, stalk and all! The regimental toast is then drunk, in absolute silence; after this, the Drum Corps march round the table before departing for their own quarters, the last man out of the mess being ritually 'captured' and then called upon to drink the officers' health before being released to rejoin his companions.

Pageantry? Well, this is not truly a public spectacle, for it is restricted to the officers and other ranks of one North Country regiment. But it does possess the essential ingredients of colour and movement, and it is marked by ritual procedure, an element fundamental to almost every traditional occasion, important or lowly, anywhere in the year-long calendar.

The Royal Navy of course has its celebrations, not the least interesting of which is the one held annually on 21st October, 'Trafalgar Day' – perhaps the best-known naval victory in our history after Drake's defeat of the Spanish Armada in 1588. Rightly, the setting is Trafalgar Square, dominated by the giant statue of Admiral Lord Nelson on the top of his 167-foot high granite column. The ceremony was instituted in 1895, when the Navy League first honoured Nelson by placing a wreath of bay leaves at the foot of his column.

Since that date the occasion has become more and more elaborate. Not only the British branch of the Navy League but branches from various Commonwealth countries take part, and also units from a number of individual ships, marines, commandos, submariners and others. Wreaths from all these units are placed round the huge plinth of the column, between the bronze lions *couchant* which Landseer designed and beneath the plaques cast from metal from French guns seized after the action in 1805. One special place is reserved every year for a wreath of laurel leaves in the form of an anchor: the specific tribute from descendants of the men who actually fought at the Battle of Trafalgar. This is certainly a truly public occasion, for Trafalgar Square is the meeting-place *par excellence* of Londoners and of visitors from overseas. How many of them, one wonders, know that the octagonal lamps to be seen at each corner of this famous square once illuminated Nelson's own flagship, *H.M.S. Victory?*

Army, Navy and Air Force come together in combined pageantry and rivalry each year at the popular Royal Tournament, for long held either at Earl's Court or at Olympia. This splendid spectacle had its modest inception way back in 1880, when certain army units and individual soldiers assembled to compete against one another with the hand weapons of the day – lances, swords and bayonets among others – and so demonstrate their individual skill and prowess. For many years past, however, it has been developed and elaborated, more and more units being introduced, each with some specific function or aptitude, until now it may be regarded as a mirror of life in the armed forces. Giant guns are manhandled over the most formidable obstacles; powerful vehicles of many kinds and uses are manoeuvred with consummate skill and impressive delicacy of touch, performing miracles of complex evolutions, by men at the wheel apparently 'driving blind'.

Martial music, of course, provides the background, and the uniforms of the many units add richness of colour that contrasts strongly with the functional battledress of the men actually engaged in feats of strength, skill and endurance that are an eloquent tribute to their fitness, keenness and expertise. Though the various manoeuvres and small-unit 'acts' may be specifically laid on by members of one or other of the armed services, an element of intense competitiveness is always present, and in such strength as to be almost palpable.

Pageantry demonstrated in one form or another by soldiers, sailors and airmen may, as we have seen, be linked with Royal Occasions or be peculiar to the service essentially involved. Inevitably there are those who maintain that such demonstrations indirectly glorify war and can even serve as a means of encouraging young men to 'take the Queen's Shilling'. They may be right. But the essential element in all these occasions, whether daily (as at Buckingham Palace and Whitehall's Changing of the Guard) or annually (as on Trafalgar and Minden Day), is the maintaining of traditions, something so deep-rooted in us all that however much circumstances continue to change, we persist in adhering to them. Even during the Second World War many of them were carried through, even if on a somewhat modified scale, rather than allow a cherished tradition to lapse.

An interesting example of a tradition that is maintained even though it lacks the spur that is obviously provided by the presence of a large audience is the one known as the Ceremony of the Keys, performed nightly at the Tower of London. Only with express permission may it be witnessed, and then only by a handful. It has taken place every night of the year for over seven centuries: perhaps the most outstanding example of a tradition that simply refuses to lie down and die.

The most spectacular civic event in Britain, the Lord Mayor's Show, is for most people the finest example of pageantry they ever witness. Here is tradition exemplified on the truly grand scale, a tradition that dates back almost exactly 600 years. And quite apart from its sheer splendour, there is an inexhaustible wealth of minor detail which, once known, can add enormously to the impact of the whole. For instance, the 400-year-old Chain of Office worn by the Lord Mayor is almost six feet in length and among its lavish embellishments are no fewer than 14 Tudor roses, 13 knots and – perhaps somewhat sinisterly – a single portcullis. Again, the magnificently groomed and caparisoned Shire horses that draw his gilded coach and are thus used only on this one annual occasion and on the occasion when a new monarch is crowned, are in fact dray-horses owned and used by a City brewery.

Another annual occasion when London's Lord Mayor is the dominating figure is the official opening of the Central Criminal Court – better known to most people as the Old Bailey. But on this occasion, though the Lord Mayor is the First Citizen of London and presides over the ceremony, for once his function is to act as escort – to the High Court Judge in his scarlet robes.

He is not, however, present at the traditional piece of subdued pageantry known as the Court of Arches. This is essentially an ecclesiastical occasion: the appointment of a new bishop to a bishopric that has fallen vacant either through the death of its incumbent or because of his translation to some other bishopric. The Queen, as *Fidei Defensor*, must be consulted by her Prime Minister, who then consults the two Archbishops; the candidate receives the recommendation of the Dean and Chapter that he be elected, and there follows the solemn ceremony. It is known as the Court of Arches because centuries ago it was carried out in the crypt of St Mary-le-Bow in the City of London, beneath the arches of Wren's church. Naturally the element of colour is subdued and that of movement relatively slight; but there are processions, and the ecclesiastical robes and the stylised ritual of Litany reading, exchange of documents and careful scrutiny and ornate signatures to schedules all constitute the true quality of pageantry, and in wholly appropriate guise.

A good illustration of the way in which tradition has been maintained over the centuries is to be found in the fact that of the 100 and more Trade or Craft Guilds that flourished in medieval times no fewer than 75 still exist. Each has its customs and rituals, its traditional rules (and penalties for their infringement), its meeting-place of lesser or greater glory. They still use their old, proud designations: Vintners, Clothworkers, Salters, Haberdashers, Merchant Taylors, Goldsmiths, Mercers, Skinners, Dyers, and so forth; and the hierarchy within each Guild is jealousy guarded.

The Livery Banquet of the Worshipful Company of Skinners, on the eve of Corpus Christi, is one of the outstanding pieces of Guild Pageantry among many; it bears an evocative title: the Cocks & Caps Ceremony. The 'cocks' of the title are in fact a set of silver-gilt drinking-cups dating from 1598 and shaped to resemble heraldic chanticleers, each standing on a base sculpted to the form of a turtle. The ritual is complex and almost as precise as a military evolution. Indeed, it is carried out to music played by the band of the Coldstream Guards. Clerk, Beadles and ten Liverymen, all suitably robed and bearing alternately a cock and a cap, process round the table at which the Master Skinner is seated with his guests. The caps, each in turn, are 'tried' on the Master Skinner Elect, the First, the Second and the Third Wardens Elect, and the Renter Warden Elect, until each cap fits and the candidate's health has been ceremonially drunk. Private pageantry, if you will – in that, unlike the Lord Mayor's Show and so many other great occasions, it cannot be witnessed by all who care to attend. But again it is a microcosm of that all-important feature of the nation's heritage, the preserving of jealously guarded traditions against the steady and, some would say, irresistible encroachment of commercialism.

Almost all the examples of traditional pageantry mentioned so far have been associated with London. But pageantry in greater or lesser degree is still to be found throughout the country; and not merely in provincial towns but in rural districts. One or two of the small towns may be mentioned first.

Knutsford, in Cheshire – the 'Cranford' of Mrs Gaskell's novel – has its Royal May Day Festival, during which the May Queen is crowned and rides in a State Coach expressly loaned for the annual occasion by the Lord Mayor of Liverpool. High Wycombe, in Buckinghamshire, has its Mayoral Weigh-in. Lichfield, the small cathedral city in Staffordshire and birthplace of Dr Samuel Johnson, has its annual Greenhill Bower Ceremony, when the colour derives largely from the masses of flowers on display. But the element of pageantry derives from the thirteenth-century Court of Arraye of Men & Arms, remembered today, seven centuries later, by a parade of citizenry in armour and bearing the weaponry of the Middle Ages. Fancy Dress worn by the younger citizens enhances the colour and variety of the spectacle.

The traditions which are maintained primarily in rural areas tend to belong to the summer season. Morris Dancing, for instance, at Bampton, Oxfordshire, and elsewhere in the country; Sword Dancing in the village of North Skelton in Yorkshire and again elsewhere; the Horn Dancing at

Abbots Bromley, Staffordshire, in the first week in September; and so on.

Can occasions such as these be called examples of true pageantry? They have colour, and movement – movement very much more pronounced than that of the stately processions and military evolutions already mentioned. They do not have the element of magnificence, but they do, many of them, compensate for this by their undoubted antiquity. Indeed, the origins of many of these ceremonies date back so far in time as to derive from pre-Christian rituals, fertility rites and associated religio-superstitious cults. These are some of the borderline examples hinted at earlier.

So too is the ceremony of the election and crowning of the May Queen among her assembled Court. It is combined with that of dancing round the Maypole, a tradition still maintained far and wide across the country, from Kingsteignton in Devon to Barwick-in-Elmet in Yorkshire. Nowhere is it to be seen better than in the tiny village of Ickwell Green, in Bedfordshire. This May Ceremony – held, unusually, towards the end of the month instead of on May Day – is colourful enough to satisfy the most exacting, and certainly there is all the movement one could ask for!

The maypole is 70 feet high and painted in the traditional spiral bands of colour from top to toe. From part way up, a couple of dozen or so wide coloured ribbons hang down. The lower ends of these are individually held by boys and girls of the village attired in old-fashioned garb – the girls in flounced skirts and 'mob' caps, the boys in smocks such as the old-time shepherds wore. Holding the ribbon ends, they dance clockwise round the pole, interweaving among themselves in a highly intricate pattern of steps so that in due course the coloured streamers are plaited into a sort of light canopy above their heads which eventually closes about the maypole to form a bright sheath for the first ten of its seventy feet from ground level.

The dancing round the maypole is accompanied by various types of traditional side-play (such as also accompanies many versions of the Morris Dancing). There are two 'Moggies', for instance, fantastically garbed and armed with besoms which are used to persuade the spectators to drop coins into their collecting-boxes. The fact that the proceedings are attended by a 'Queen' – who must always be a local girl – and her Court endows them with a certain sense of 'occasion'. It is also a reminder that in the Middle Ages, and certainly in Tudor times, the maypole ceremonies were frequently attended by the reigning monarch and members of his or her court.

It is ceremonies such as this, the Morris, Sword and Horn Dancing, the so-called Common Ridings, as at Hawick and Selkirk in Scotland – a form of Beating the Bounds – all in rural rather than urban settings, that make the selecting of examples of Pageantry, as ordinarily understood, something of a problem. There is only one criterion truly common to those about which there is no question (those, in fact, which are described and illustrated in the pages that follow) and to those borderline examples that may be rejected by the purist. This criterion is, of course, Tradition.

Any form of ceremonial, indoors or outdoors, in town or city or country-side, with or without the processional element, literally or only figuratively 'colourful', may justifiably be termed Pageantry, at least in its widest con-notation, provided it is rooted in this deeply felt and jealously guarded prerequisite. The total number of occasions of this sort in Britain runs not just into scores but into many hundreds. Some are vastly older than others; some are vastly more eye-catching than others; all possess individual qualities with peculiar appeal to assorted tastes. Just occasionally there is an example of Pageantry at its finest that has some claim to uniqueness; one such occurred in 1965.

Not since the State Funeral of the Duke of Wellington, 113 years earlier, had London staged a comparable spectacle. The occasion was the funeral of Sir Winston Churchill: a never-to-be-forgotten experience for the thousands privileged to witness it. Not the least memorable feature of the ceremonial was its final stage, when the pageant of his passing was set on the waters of the Thames, traditionally London's great highway, along which monarchs have made their progresses and their enemies have been conveyed to the Traitors' Gate at the Tower of London. The occasion was ample proof (if proof were needed) that even in this increasingly materialistic age Britain possesses the capability and the imagination to produce Pageantry that can hold its own with any that has been witnessed down the long centuries of her history.

LONDON: FOUNDER'S DAY AT THE ROYAL HOSPITAL, CHELSEA

This beautiful building, by Sir Christopher Wren, is the home of the Chelsea Pensioners, aged veteran soldiers in retirement, founded (it is said) at the instigation of the king's mistress, Nell Gwynne, by Charles II three centuries ago. Annually on 'Oak Apple Day', the anniversary of his birthday, the 400 Royal Pensioners assemble in the principal court, attired in their picturesque scarlet frock coats and cocked hats, to parade before some member of the Royal Family. Every pensioner wears a sprig of oak, to commemorate Charles II's hiding in the famous Boscobel Oak after his defeat by the Roundheads at the Battle of Worcester, on his actual birthday in 1651.

A brief, formal address is delivered. This is followed by the traditional three cheers given twice: first for 'Our Pious Founder, King Charles' and then for 'Her Majesty the Queen'. While martial music is played in the Figure Court, the Royal Hospital is officially inspected. Then the general public may inspect it also. But by then the pensioners have settled down to the most welcome and least exacting stage in the day's celebrations (for many of them are men in their eighties and even nineties): the welcome meal of plum-duff washed down with a pint of beer.

Chelsea Royal Hospital, une des réalisations de Wren, abrite 400 pensionnaires, des soldats retraités. Le jour de l'anniversaire du fondateur Charles II, les pensionnaires, vêtus de leur habit écarlate et de leur chapeau à cornes, se rassemblent dans la cour pour défiler devant un membre de la Famille Royale.

Dieses wunderbare unter Wren erbaute Gebäude ist das Heim der Chelsea-Pensionäre, ausgediente Soldaten. Es wurde vor 300 Jahren erbaut, und am Jahrestag der Geburt Karl II., dem Grüder, versammeln sich die Veteranen in ihren malerischen Uniformen auf dem Hauptplatz, um eine Parade vor Mitgliedern der königlichen Familie abzuhalten.

LONDON: THE QUEEN'S BIRTHDAY SALUTE

This is one of the most dramatic and impressive of all small-scale royal-military ceremonies. It takes place in Hyde Park on 21 April, and also on the anniversaries of the Queen's Accession and Coronation. The arrival of the King's Troop of the Royal Horse Artillery is spectacular: six 13-pounder guns, each drawn by six horses with three riders. The guns first went into service in 1904, and were last used in action in 1942.

In overall command is a Major, as Commanding Officer. Each two-gun section is commanded by a Captain or a Lieutenant, and each gun sub-section consists of a Sergeant and a gun detachment of three men. Officers and men alike wear full dress. This consists of a black fur busby with a red bag, white plume and yellow lines, a blue jacket frogged in yellow with a red collar, blue pantaloons with a red stripe, spurred black boots and white gloves.

The Royal Salute consists of 41 rounds, fired at 10-second intervals, the first round being fired at 11 o'clock, the exact moment when Her Majesty arrives on Horse Guards Parade for the Trooping of the Colour. The manoeuvring of the horses and guns and the firing which follows are carried out with extreme military precision controlled by an elaborate code of commands given by the Major in supreme charge of the whole operation.

Ceci est une des cérémonies militaires les plus impressionnantes; elle a lieu dans Hyde Park, le 21 avril, jour de l'anniversaire de la Reine. Le "Royal Salute" consiste de 41 coups de canon, tirés à 10 secondes d'intervalle, à partir de 11 heures précises.

Eine der eindrucksvollsten Militärparaden ist der königliche Geburtstags-salut, der jährlich am 21. April im Hyde Park stattfindet. Bei Ankuft der Königin, um die Fahnenparade abzuhalten, werden 41 Salven in Abständen von 10 Sekunden abgefeuert.

STRATFORD-UPON-AVON: SHAKESPEARE'S BIRTHDAY COMMEMORATION

Shakespeare is believed to have been born, and known to have died, on 23 April; that date is the high spot of the annual Shakespeare Festival, which in fact lasts from April to October. It is attended by drama lovers from all over the world; evidence of the universality of the cult appears in the multitudinous national flags lining Bridge Street on flagstaffs bearing heraldic shields 'opened' by representatives of those nations following the 'breaking' at midday of the Union Jack on the main flagstaff, while the bells of Holy Trinity Church, where Shakespeare was baptised in 1564 and buried in 1616, ring out over the thronged town.

After this, a public Birthday lunch organised by the Shakespeare Club is given in the Conference Hall; the banks of the Avon, which flows past the Memorial Theatre, are crowded with sightseers; many of the town's streets are closed save to pedestrians; there are pilgimages to his birthplace in Henley Street; wreaths and, especially, posies of 'Rosemary for Remembrance' are laid on his grave, to which the mayor leads a procession of dignitaries in homage. Anne Hathaway's Cottage, at near-by Shottery, is also a place of pilgrimage. It is seen here with a troop of Morris Dancers who assemble there on May Day, one week after the Bard of Avon's birthday.

Les amateurs de théâtre se rassemblent ici le 23 avril: des drapeaux de tous les pays du monde pavoisent Bridge Street, les cloches de Holy Trinity Church sonnent, des gerbes sont déposées sur la tombe de Shakespeare; le pélérinage comprend aussi un défilé jusqu'à la chaumière de Ann Hathaway, que l'on voit ici; Un groupe de "Morris Dancers" s'y rassemble le jour du 1er mai.

Stratford-upon-Avon ist der Wallfahrtsort aller Shakespeareliebhaber, wo jedes Jahr die Shakespeare-Festspiele stattfinden und deren Höhepunkt jährlich der Todestag des Dichters ist. Das Haus seiner Gemahlin Anne Hathaway ist ebenso ein Wallfahrtsort, wo sich immer am 1. Mai eine Tanzgruppe einfindet.

LONDON: CORONATION OF THE MONARCH

The ritual crowning of the new monarch in Westminster Abbey is exceedingly elaborate. Seated in the Coronation Chair, first used by Edward II in 1308 and containing the historic 'Stone of Scone', the monarch is annointed by the Archbishop of Canterbury and thus 'consecrated Sovereign to his/her High Office'. There follows the investiture with the Royal Robes and Insignia: the Spurs; the Sovereign's Sword – then placed on the altar 'in the Service of God'; the Orb – 'Symbol of Sovereignty under the Cross'; the Ring – 'of Kingly Dignity and the Seal of Catholic Faith'; the Royal Sceptre – 'Ensign of Kingly Power and Justice'; the Rod with the Dove – 'Rod of Equity and Mercy'. Finally St Edward's Crown – 'Emblem of Glory, Honour and Courage' – is taken from the altar and placed on the Sovereign's head by the Archbishop.

The Sovereign then moves to another seat, on a raised daïs, to receive homage. Elizabeth II is seen here wearing the St Edward's Crown, later to be replaced by the Imperial State Crown. On her right stands the Bishop of Durham (now Archbishop of Canterbury); on her left stands the Bishop of Bath and Wells; since the coronation of Richard I these bishops have had the hereditary right to 'support' the newly-crowned monarch. The bare-headed figure below the daïs is the then Archbishop of Canterbury; the kneeling figure is the Duke of Edinburgh, paying homage as Consort to the Queen.

Cette cérémonie extrêmement raffinée, a lieu à l'Abbaye de Westminster. Ici, Elizabeth II porte la couronne de St Edward; à sa droite se tient l'évêque de Durham, à sa gauche l'évêque de Bath et de Wells; la personne nu-tête au-dessous du dais, est l'Archevêque de Canterbury d'alors, la personne agenouillée est le Duc d'Edinbourg, rendant hommage à la Reine.

Die Krönung eines neuen Monarchen ist eine äusserst komplizierte Zeremonie, die jeweils in der Westminster Abtei stattfindet. Hier wird der Monarch zunächst von dem Erzbischof von Canterbury gesalbt. Das Bild zeigt Königin Elisabeth II. mit der Sankt-Eduard-Krone, die später durch die Reichskrone ersetzt wird.

LONDON: CEREMONY OF THE KEYS

Probably the oldest military ceremony in the world, this has been carried out nightly at the Tower of London for more than 700 years. At seven minutes to ten, a sergeant of the Guards with four other ranks, in dress uniform and carrying bayonet-set rifles, present themselves in turn at the four main towers. At the Bloody Tower they are challenged: 'Halt! Who comes there?' On receiving the response, 'The Keys', the sentry demands: 'Whose Keys?' The response comes promptly: 'Queen Elizabeth's Keys'. 'Pass, Queen Elizabeth's Keys. All's well!' comes the command.

The Guards' Escort of the Keys passes through the archway to the Main Guard. Arms are presented, as a military salute to the Keys and the Chief Warder doffs his hat and cries: 'God preserve Queen Elizabeth!', to which the Escort of The Keys reply in unison, 'Amen!' The timing of this age-old ceremony is so precise that as the word is spoken the hour of ten strikes; this is the cue for the Tower Bugler to sound the traditional Last Post. All that remains to do is for the Chief Warder to convey the Queen's Keys to the Resident Governor in what, since this was once a monarch's City Residence, is known today as The Queen's House.

La cérémonie militaire probablement la plus vieille du monde, est exécutée chaque soir depuis plus de 700 ans à la Tour de Londres. Des gardes réclament les "Keys" de la Reine Elizabeth. Il est 10 heures et l'on entend la dernière partie de la sonnerie traditionnelle.

Dies ist wohl eine der ältesten Militärzeremonien der Welt, die hier im Tower von London seit über 700 Jahren ausgetragen wird. Im Bloody Tower überreichen die vier Wachoffiziere dem Beefeater die sogenannten 'königlichen Schlüssel', der diese nach einemzeremoniellen Anruf entgegennimmt und dem Residenzgouverneur überreicht.

LONDON: DISTRIBUTION OF THE ROYAL MAUNDY

The distributing of this 'dole' dates back more than 600 years and takes place annually on the day before Good Friday. Alternately in Westminster Abbey and some other prominent cathedral or church, usually in London or Windsor, the reigning monarch, attended by the Yeomen of the Guard and the Archbishop of Canterbury as Lord High Almoner, or some other high ecclesiast, and a procession of dignitaries and clergy, meets a number of men and women equal to the tally of her own years.

White and red purses carried on a tray by a Yeoman of the Guard contain specially minted small coins amounting to a sum that, again, tallies with the monarch's age; these are distributed personally to the recipients lined up on each side, one of each colour to each in turn. Nowadays the purses contain coins to the value of approximately £5, but such is the rarity of these small silver coins, minted to the equivalent of one, two, three and four pence, that collectors will gladly pay substantially over the odds to the rare recipient prepared to part with his or her Royal Gift. A small picturesque feature of this antique ceremony is the carrying by members of the procession of little nosegays of flowers: a reminder that this was common practice in such ceremonies, and in courts of law, to combat, it was hoped, the risk of infection from proximity to people of low degree.

Depuis 600 ans, chaque année, à l'abbaye de Westminster ou autre église, à Londres ou à Windsor, la veille du Vendredi Saint, le monarque suivi de Beefeaters, de l'archevêque de Canterbury, et d'un cortège de dignitaires et membres du clergé, rencontre un groupe d'hommes et de femmes auxquels sont distribuées des bourses contenant de petites pièces d'argent spécialement frappées.

Dieser 600 Jahre alte Brauch findet jährlich einen Tag vor Karfreitag in der Westminster Abtei oder einer anderen bekannten Kirche statt. Der regierende Monarch, in Begleitung des Leibgardisten und anderen Würdenträgern, übergibt einer auserwählten Zahl von Leuten speziell für diesen Anlass geprägte Münzen, deren Anzahl mit dem Alter des Monarchen übereinstimmt.

OXFORD: ENCAENIA

This most impressive occasion in the scholastic world is rightly held in our oldest university: it is the day on which honorary degrees are awarded to a number of very distinguished personalities in various spheres and from various countries. It takes place in the second half of June, on the Wednesday of the ninth week of the Trinity Full Term.

Oxford's 'Noblemen, Heads of Houses, Doctors, Proctors and Gentlemen' are summoned to meet the Chancellor in the Vice-Chancellor's college. Thence a procession headed by the Chancellor in his black-and-gold robe, its train borne by a formally attired scholar, and consisting in strict traditional order of Doctors of Theology, of Medicine, of Law and of Music, followed by the Proctors, Presidents and Provosts, makes its way to the Sheldonian Theatre. It includes those about to be honoured, wearing their newly acquired academic robes, the University Registrar and the Public Orator. After the National Anthem has been played, the Chancellor touches his gold-tasselled cap and makes his initial pronouncement. Then, with extreme formality, the individual degrees are bestowed upon the honorands, while the Public Orator declaims a brief eulogy of each – in Latin, as befits so ancient a foundation as Oxford University.

Dans notre plus vieille université, en juin, le jour où l'on décerne des grades honorifiques à un certain nombre de personnalités de marque, les dignitaires scholastiques d'Oxford et le Chancelier de l'université se dirigent vers Sheldonian Theatre. Les grades sont accordés individuellement, pendant que l'Orateur fait une éloge en latin.

Einer der eindrucksvollsten Anlässe der akademischen Welt findet mit Recht in unserer ältesten Universität an dem Tage statt, an dem Ehrendoktortitel an berühmte Persönlichkeiten des In- und Auslandes verliehen werden. Bei der Zeremonie hält der öffentliche Redner bei der Verleihung eines jeden Titels eine kurze Lobrede – in latein natürlich.

LONDON: DOGGETT'S COAT AND BADGE RACE

This river event, said to be the oldest rowing race in the world, takes place annually on the Thames on or about 1 August. The starting-point is Old Swan Pier, London Bridge, and the men row upstream to the site of the Old White Swan, close by Chelsea Bridge. The winner of the race (there are six contestants), instituted by Thomas Doggett in 1716 in honour of the accession of George 1 on 1 August and carried out almost without a break ever since, is rewarded with 'an Orange Livery Jacket with a Silver Badge representing Liberty on the left Arm thereof'. Formerly orange, it is now scarlet, with silver buttons, and the silver badge carries the emblem of the House of Hanover, a White Horse, together with the word Liberty.

The competitors are all watermen who have just completed their apprenticeship, which means that they have only one chance in a lifetime of competing. The men are followed by a barge containing a number of previous winners, each man wearing his well-earned scarlet quilted jacket, matched with old-style breeches, silk stockings and buckled shoes and the picturesque headgear of the period. Here we see past winners and the traditionally dressed watermen of the various Companies involved in Doggett's Coat-and-Badge race: from left to right, the Vintners' Company; Fishmongers' Company; the Queen's Bargemaster; the Company of Watermen and Lightermen; the Dyers' Company.

Cette course d'aviron se passe, chaque année, depuis 1716, au début d'août, sur la Tamise, entre Old Swan Pier et Old White Swan; les candidats sont des mariniers qui viennent de finir leur apprentissage; le gagnant reçoit un veston écarlate, aux boutons d'argent, orné d'une médaille d'argent, veston qu'il portera chaque année le jour de la course.

Eine der ältesten Ruderveranstaltungen der Welt, die jährlich am 1. August auf der Themse ausgetragen wird. Sie wurde zuerst von Thomas Doggett im Jahre 1716 zu Ehren der Thronfolge Georg 1. eingeleitet und wird von Flussschiffern ausgetragen, die soeben ihre Lehrzeit beendet haben. Dem Sieger wird eine orangenfarbige Zunftjacke mit einem Silberabzeichen überreicht.

STONEHENGE: MIDSUMMER EVE DRUID RITES

This age-old ritual possesses a haunting quality unmatched anywhere else in Britain. On Midsummer Eve the members of the Ancient Order of Druid Hermetists assemble among the enormous trilithons of local 'sarsens' and the 'bluestones' from distant Prescelly that constitute the most impressive of all our existing prehistoric monuments, to keep their traditional vigil throughout the night which culminates in the rising of the sun witnessed between two of the monoliths and over the so-called 'Hele', or Sun, Stone on Midsummer Day.

The Druids, garbed in white robes, carrying ornate banners embroidered with mystic symbols, process among the towering stones, led by the Arch, or Chief, Druid. They reach the so-called 'Altar Stone', believed to have been the focal point of pagan sun-worship. At sunrise a ritual Solstice Service is held, the Druid Priest intoning a declaration which begins: 'God, our All-Father, permanent amid all change art Thou', and ends with the solemn words: 'The sleep of Faith has ever led through night to dawn'. His 'Amen' is taken up by all the Druids present; and indeed by the vast congregation that, without fail, assembles each year to take part in the solemn ceremony.

La veille du Solstice d'été, les membres de l'Ancien Ordre des Druides se rassemblent parmi les trilithes, qui constituent les monuments préhistoriques les plus impressionnants, pour veiller toute la nuit, jusqu'à ce que le soleil se lève; les druides éxécutent alors les rites de la cérémonie du Solstice.

Uraltes Ritual, das kaum irgendwo auf der Insel seinesgleichen findet. Am Abend des Johannistages versammeln sich Mitgleider des alten Ordens der Druid Hermetists an diesem vorhistorischen Monument, wo sie ihre traditionelle Nachwache bis zum Sonnenaufgang halten. Der Altarstein ist der Mittelpunkt der Sonnenanbetung.

LONDON: STATE OPENING OF PARLIAMENT

The formal opening of each new parliamentary session takes place in the first week of November: an occasion of great ceremony and solemn ritual. The monarch arrives in the sumptuous Irish State Coach, escorted by a unit of the Household Cavalry, to be welcomed by the Earl Marshal, the Lord Chancellor and the Lord Great Chamberlain. Prior to her arrival, ever mindful of Guy Fawkes's attempt in 1605 to blow up Parliament, the vaults are ceremonially searched by the Yeomen of the Guard in their Tudor costumes. Meanwhile, the Imperial State Crown, the Sword of Maintenance and the Cap of State have been brought from the Palace of St James to the Royal Robing Room at the House of Lords.

Robed and crowned, the monarch enters the Upper House, thronged with Peers, Diplomats, Bishops, Judges, and their Ladies, all wearing such regalia as their offices permit. Having ascended the Throne, she summons the Loyal Commons. The officer known as Black Rod conveys the command, and M.P.s, headed by the Speaker, Prime Minister and Leader of the Opposition, file in to take their places before the Bar of the House. The monarch then proceeds to read the Speech from the Throne (as seen in our picture), a formal document outlining her government's future policies. The speech ended, Parliament is then officially open.

La première semaine de novembre le monarque ouvre la nouvelle session parlementaire; le monarque convoque les membres du parlement, et fait un discours. Avant l'arrivée du monarque, on fouille les caves du Parlement, pour ne pas oublier la tentative de Guy Fawkes de faire sauter le Parlement en 1605.

Die offiziellen Eröffnung einer neuen Parlamentsperiode findet jeweils in der ersten Novemberwoche statt. Bei diesem äusserst wichtigen und ernsten Ritual ist der Monarch zugegen. Hier verliesst die Königin eine Rede vom Thron, in der die zukünftige Politik der Regierung in groben Zügen dargestellt wird. Nach Beendigung dieser Zeremonie ist das Parlament offiziell eröffnet.

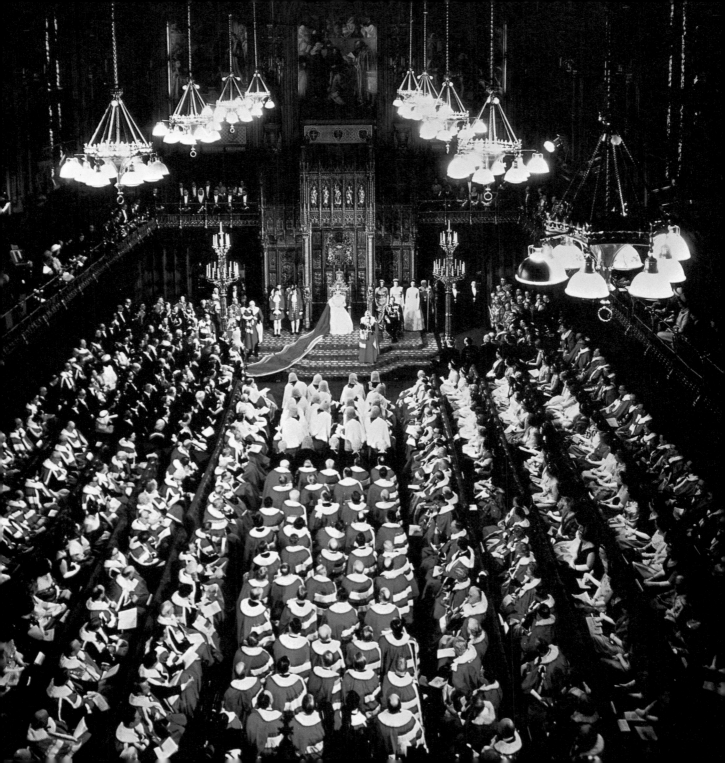

SANDHURST: THE SOVEREIGN'S PARADE

Held usually in the last week of July, this is the most memorable as well as brilliant occasion in the life of cadets training at the Royal Military Academy, the culmination of two years' intensive work in class-room and on parade-ground. It fuses the annual passing-out parades held, until a quarter-century ago, at both Sandhurst and Woolwich. The whole college assembles to witness the moment when the senior officer cadets parade for the last time before receiving their Sovereign's Commissions.

The Colour is escorted by them as they march past, the salute being taken by the monarch or a suitably distinguished representative. This Trooping of the Colour is followed by an address. Then, the coveted Sword of Honour is presented to the cadet regarded by the college authorities as the outstanding cadet of his 'term', a decision always based on all-round performance, character and calibre rather than on purely academic attainment. The Monarch's Medal is a second highly coveted award, made to a second cadet on a different basis of selection. Finally this Senior Division marches from the parade-ground and up the wide steps to the Grand Entrance, to the tune of 'Auld Lang Syne' played by the band. The climax comes when, by tradition, the Adjutant follows them, on horseback, up the steps and into the Royal Military College itself.

Après deux années d'entraînement intense à la Royal Military Academy, le bataillon scolaire défile pour la dernière fois, devant tout le collège assemblé, avant de recevoir leur Brevet du Souverain. Une présentation de drapeaux est suivie d'une allocution, puis, le Souverain présente des récompenses très convoitées aux meilleurs élèves.

Dies ist einer der denkwürdigsten und glänzendsten Anlässe im Leben eines jeden jungen Kadetten, der auf der Königlichen Militärakademie Sandhurst ausgebildet wird und ist der Höhepunkt einer intensiven zweijährigen Ausbildung. Die Parade endet, indem der Adjutant zu Pferd einer Division Rangältester in das Royal Military College folgt.

LONDON: CHANGING OF THE GUARD AT BUCKINGHAM PALACE

This ceremony takes place daily when the monarch is in residence – as indicated by the fact that the Royal Standard will be flying. Shortly before eleven o'clock each morning, in the Fore Court, the New Guard, in dress uniform, preceded by the Guards' Band, advances towards the old Guard to the music of the appropriate regimental slow march. The ritual drill that leads up to the actual change-over is complicated and performed with absolute precision. A junior officer of the regiment involved carries the Regimental Colour, to which, if the day happens to be an anniversary of some battle in which the regiment fought, by custom a laurel wreath is attached.

There follows a formal exchange of military courtesies, clicking of heels and presenting of arms on both sides. While the new sentries are being posted, the officers, in a strictly determined hierarchy, march up and down in pairs, while the band continues to play. The sentries who have been relieved smartly rejoin the other members of the assembled Old Guard, and march out of the main gateway of the Fore Court, still to the regimental slow march. This is changed to the regimental quick march as soon as the men set foot on the roadway beyond the railings.

Cette cérémonie a lieu chaque matin, un peu avant 11 heures, quand le monarque est au Palais; (dans ce cas, le drapeau royal flottera) la nouvelle Garde, en uniforme d'apparat, précédée de la musique de la Garde, vient relever l'ancienne Garde.

Die Wachablösung findet täglich statt, wenn sich der Monarch im Buckingham-Palast aufhält. Dies geschieht kurz vor 11 Uhr morgens im Vorhof, wenn die neue Wache in Begleitung eines Militärmarsches aufzieht, um die alte Wache abzulösen. Danach erfolgt die formelle militärische Begrüssung.

THE THAMES: SWAN-UPPING

Because by long tradition the swan has always been regarded as a royal bird, a licence was necessary to own one. Queen Elizabeth I granted two exceptions: to the Vintners' and the Dyers' Livery Companies. Annually, towards the end of July, all the swans on the Thames between Henley and London Bridge are ceremonially checked. The cygnets born during the past 12 months – often as many as 500 and more – must be located and, unless they are the offspring of the monarch's swans, must have their beaks nicked, or 'upped', according to whether they belong to the Vintners or the Dyers. The procedure may well take many days, or even a week or two.

The Queen's Swan-Keeper, or Master, wears scarlet livery, with a feather behind his cap badge; he commands the convoy of skiffs. One of these carries the Dyers' Swan-Master, in blue livery; another carries the Vintners' Swan-Master, in livery of green. All the skiffs bear the royal and national colours of red, white and blue, and these colours may also be carried in the striped woollen jerseys worn by the oarsmen, all of whom have the respective badges of their office embroidered across their chests. White trousers and, often, woolly caps complete their traditional apparel.

Par tradition, les cygnes appartiennent au Souverain, ou à la Corporation des Négociants en vins ou à celle des Teinturiers. En juillet, entre Henley et London Bridge, a lieu le recensement des cygnes: les représentants de ces 3 groupes cherchent les jeunes afin de les marquer.

Aufgrund langer Tradition sind Schwäne immer als ein majestätische Vögel angesehen worden, die, mit Ausnahme der Weinhändler- und Färberzünften seit Elisabeth I. dem Monarchen gehören. Jährlich werden die Sohwäne auf der Themse zwischen Henley und London Bridge überprüft. Die Jungen müssen, sofern sie nicht dem Monarchen gehören, am Schnabel markiert werden.

LONDON: EASTER PARADE

Neither royal nor military, this annual example of pageantry is immensely colourful and lively; few such events so completely involve the spectator. It opens at 3 o'clock on Easter Sunday afternoon in Battersea Park, once notorious as a site for duels and also for less formal exhibitions of violence, though it became 'respectable' and was even visited by that most respectable monarch, Queen Victoria. Since that occasion it has become more and more the *venue* for the display of the latest (and often most outrageous) in feminine fashion. Here you may see, in all its traditional extravagance, the 'Easter Bonnet', and all the finery that goes with it.

Here too you may see, in the tradition of the Jersey and Nice and other Carnivals, the flower-bedecked floats carrying tableaux representing historic and picturesque scenes involving pretty girls, grotesque larger-than-life creatures, ornamental objects that might be wedding-cake decorations on an outsize scale. There is music from the bands; there are the Pearly Kings and their even more lavishly bejewelled Queens; there are circus characters both two-legged and four-legged. Indeed, there is everything that young and old alike could possibly demand for an Easter Sunday afternoon's entertainment.

Pittoresque et plein de vie, ce défilé, le jour de Pâques, commence dans Battersea Park. Vous y verrez les chars traditionnels aux carnivals, représentant des scènes historiques ou pittoresques, mêlant jolies filles, créatures grotesques, et objets de tailles exceptionnelle, les fanfares, les "Pearly Kings" et des personnages et animaux de cirque.

Die Osterparade ist weder ein militärischer noch ein königlicher Anlass. Sie beginnt am Nachmittag des Ostersonntag im Battersea Park und könnte mit den traditionellen Karnevalsveranstaltungen von Jersey und Nizza verglichen werden. Im Laufe der Zeit ist dies zu einem Treffpunkt des letzten Modeschreis für die weiblichen Besucher geworden und wird sogar manchmal als frevelhaft bezeichnet.

LONDON: A STATE BANQUET IN THE GUILDHALL

This brilliant occasion is the official gesture from the Mayor, Sheriff and Aldermen of the City of London to a visiting Head of State. Guildhall, a Wren masterpiece, has for 300 years past been the home of the civic government of the City of London, of which the Lord Mayor is First Citizen. All the most notable figures in the Diplomatic Services both of Britain and of foreign countries with representatives in London attend. Church dignitaries, top brass in the armed services, and personalities who dominate public life in a wide variety of spheres: all are in this glittering galaxy of guests.

The initial reception takes place in the Guildhall Library. From there, the majority of the guests go to take their places at the tables in the Great Hall, on whose walls may be seen, in addition to the Arms of England and much other insignia, the scrolls of 600 former Lord Mayors of London. Then, a fanfare of trumpets announces the arrival of the Lord Mayor's procession, and they take their places. There are diverse toasts, and, also by tradition, the occasion is often the brilliant setting for a major political speech from the Prime Minister.

Here we see a State Banquet being given for a visiting foreign Head of State.

Guildhall, chef-d'oeuvre de l'architecte Wren, abrite depuis 300 ans le gouvernement municipal de la Cité de Londres. Lors du Banquet, qui a lieu dans le Great Hall, l'Archevêque de Canterbury porte un toast au nouveau Lord Mayor, et, par tradition, le Premier Ministre fait un discours politique important.

Bei diesem traditionellen Bankett, dass jährlich als offizielle Geste des neugewählten Oberbürgermeisters von London für seinen Vorgänger gegeben wird, findet im Beisein vieler Persönlichkeiten des Diplomatischen Corps im Rathaus der City von London statt. Es werden dabei viele Trinksprüche gehalten und hierbei bietet sich dem Premier eine ausgezeichnete Gelegenheit, eine wichtige politische Rede zu halten.

LONDON: CHANGING OF THE GUARD IN WHITEHALL

The setting for this daily ceremony is the double-arched gateway to the Horse Guards Building, the site of the Guard House to the seventeenth-century Palace of Whitehall. The Queen's Life Guard consists of 22 men when she is resident in London. They are men either from the Royal Horse Guards ('The Blues'), recognisable by their blue tunics and cloaks and red plumes in their helmets and seated on black saddle sheepskins, or from the Life Guards, who wear scarlet tunics and cloaks and white helmet plumes and are seated on white saddle sheepskins. The two regiments constitute the Household Cavalry, which provides the Sovereign's Escort for State Occasions.

The changing of this guard takes place at exactly eleven o'clock on every weekday – coinciding with that at Buckingham Palace; on Sundays the ceremonies take place one hour earlier. Of the two, many visitors find the Whitehall ceremony the more engrossing, for here, unlike the men seen in ritual action against the imposing façade of the monarch's official London residence, the outgoing guards and the men who take their places beneath the arches are mounted, and on steeds superlatively groomed and caparisoned; moreover, they may be approached so closely that one can feel the breath of the horses' nostrils on one's face!

Les Life-Guards de la Reine, appartiennent soit aux Royal Horse Guards, à l'habit bleu et au casque à plumes rouges, ou aux Life-Guards, à l'habit rouge et au casque à plumes blanches. La relève de ces gardes à cheval a lieu chaque matin à 11 heures, à la grille du bâtiment des Horse-Guards.

Der Schauplatz dieser täglichen Zeremonie ist das doppelbögige Tor der Gardekavallerie, die zum Whitehall-Palast gehört, erbaut im 17. Jhd. Die Garde besteht entweder aus Männern der königlichen Gardekavallerie oder der königlichen Leibwache und bilden die Hauskavallerie, die bei Staatbesuchen eine königliche Eskorte zur Verfügung stellen.

ISLE OF MAN: TYNWALD OPEN-AIR PARLIAMENT

This constitutional gathering dates back some ten centuries and the open-air ritual undoubtedly derives from Viking tradition. On Old Midsummer Day – 5 July – the Lieutenant-Governor of the island, the monarch's representative, proceeds in state to Tynwald Hill, reputedly man-made from the soil of the 17 parishes of the Isle of Man. In full dress uniform, attended by dignitaries of Church and State and preceded by his Sword Bearer, he passes between two lines of guardsmen, to take his seat, which always faces to the east. The thirteenth-century Sword of State is held in front of him, point upwards. He is now presiding over his Legislative Council.

This consists of the Bishop, and the Deemsters who represent the Judiciary. On a lower terrace sit the 24 Members of the House of Keys constituting the island's Parliament, believed to be the smallest in the world, and the High Bailiff and Captains of the Parishes. The Chief Justice reads out, in both English and Manx, the language of the island still spoken by the older inhabitants at least, the Acts passed by the English Parliament to which the Royal Assent has been given during the past year. Immediately following this, the 'Act of Tynwald' – a word derived from the Norse *Thing Vollr*, or 'fenced open assembly' – becomes law in the Isle of Man.

Cette assemblée constitutionnelle date d'au moins 10 siècles et dérive de la tradition viking. Le 5 juillet, le Lieutenant-Gouverneur de l'Ile de Man, préside le conseil législatif, en plein-air, sur la colline Tynwald; là, sont lus les actes passés par le Gouvernement anglais, approuvés par le Souverain.

Die konstitionellen Treffen auf der Insel Man sind Jahrhunderte alt, und dieses Freilichtparlament stammt zweifellos aus der Zeit der Vikinger. Bei dieser jährlichen Zeremonie verliesst der Hauptrichter die verschiedenen Gesetze, die vom englischen Parlament während des Vorjahres verabschiedet wurden, in Englisch und Manx.

BRAEMAR: ROYAL HIGHLAND GATHERING

This annual occasion, instituted 150 years ago by the Braemar Highland Society, received its cachet, 'Royal', when Queen Victoria attended it. It is held in Princess Royal Park, close to the monarch's Highland Seat, Balmoral, in the first week of September. Members of the Royal Family always attend, and it is certainly the most splendid annual Scottish occasion held anywhere outside Edinburgh itself.

The Highland Games are the outstanding spectacle: putting the stone, throwing the hammer, wrestling in both catch-as-catch-can and Cumberland style; but in these competitive sports the most notable feature of all is that known as 'tossing the caber'. The caber is a Scots pine log up to 20 feet in length and weighing well over a hundredweight; this the brawny, kilted competitors must 'toss' into the air. The record 'toss' was that of an outsize caber that weighed no less than 230 pounds! This is a form of combined weight-lifting and throwing that demands enormous strength and balance and arouses appropriate excitement among the beholders.

Our picture shows a Highland pipe-band, in traditional tartan, which accompanies the events and ceremonies with the stirring skirl of the bagpipes.

La Famille Royale assiste à ce spectacle grandiose, qui a lieu chaque année en septembre. Les Jeux Ecossais forment un spectacle marquant: le lancement du marteau, la lutte, le célèbre "tossing of the caber" (lancement d'un tronc de mélèze); en plus de ces sports, les danses écossaises et la musique des cornemuses ajoutent à la grandeur de cet évènement.

Die Highland Games sind wirklich der glänzendste aller schottischen Anlässe, die jährlich in Edinburg stattfinden. Hierbei werden eine Vielzahl von Wettbewerben und Spielen ausgetragen, deren Höhepunkt das Baumstammwerfen ist. Natürlich fehlt es auch nicht am musikalischen Beitrag der Dudelsäcke und dem traditionellen Volkstanz.

WALES: INVESTITURE OF THE PRINCE OF WALES AT CAERNARVON CASTLE

In 1284, Edward I presented his newly born son, Edward Plantagenet (later Edward II) to the people of Wales with the words 'Eich Dyn' ('This is your man'). These ancient words were heard again on 1 July, 1969. Against its cold grey stone moved the Queen's Bodyguards of Yeomen and Gentlemen-at-Arms; the Sovereign's Household Cavalry; the Heralds and Pursuivants-of-Arms in their brilliant liveries; Lord Snowdon, Constable of the Castle; 4,000 guests, including all the Royals, the Diplomatic Corps, Peers of the Realm, the Arch Druid and other Welsh notables; the Secretary of State for Wales and the Welsh Herald of Arms.

The supreme moment was when the heir to the throne knelt before his mother to speak the solemn oath. She had bestowed the Sword of Office, the Gold Rod, emblem of Government, the Gold Ring, and had crowned him. Now, his hands between hers, he declared: 'I, Charles, Prince of Wales, do become your liege man of life and limb and of earthly worship.' Music was played by military bands; orchestral music specially composed by the Master of the Queen's Music was also played. Penillion Singing, essentially Welsh in character, added appropriate and haunting sound to the occasion: an occasion, of course, which may well not be repeated for another half century and more.

Le Château de Caernarvon fut le site d'un déploiement de faste le 1er juillet 1969, jour où Charles fut investi en tant que Prince de Galles. C'est là que l'héritier de la Couronne s'agenouilla devant sa mère et prêta serment.

Am 1. Juli 1969 fand die Investitur des Prinz von Wales in allem Prunk in Caernarvon statt. Der Höhepunkt dieses seltenen Ereignisses war, als der Thronfolger vor seiner Mutter niederkniete, um den feierlichen Eid abzulegen.

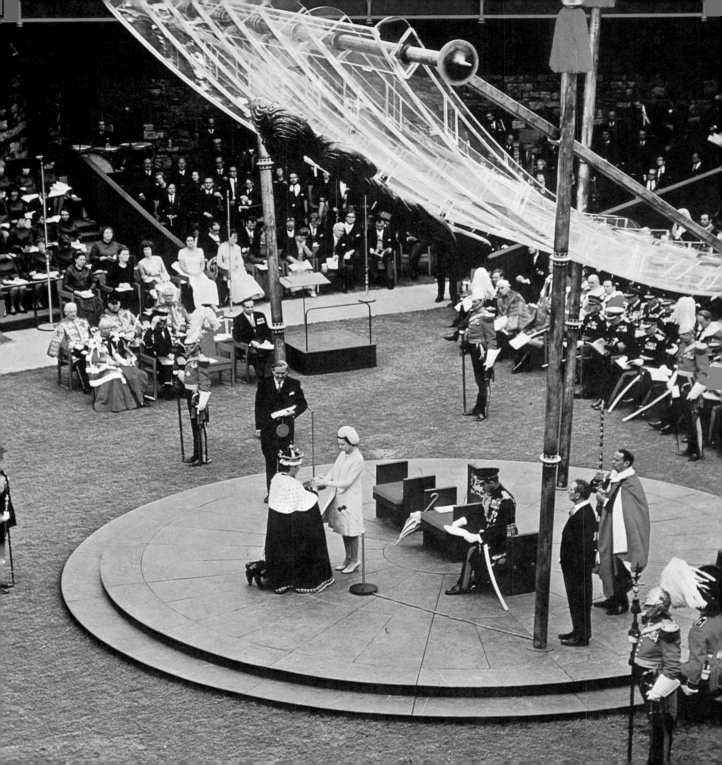

LONDON: TROOPING THE COLOUR

This superb example of military pageantry was instituted 200 years ago by George II. It takes place annually on the monarch's 'official birthday', the second Saturday in June, on the vast parade-ground just off Whitehall known as Horse Guards Parade. The monarch rides in state from Buckingham Palace, attended by the Sovereign's Mounted Escort. Awaiting her at Horse Guards are the Household Cavalry and the Brigade of Guards. As Colonel-in-Chief of several regiments, Her Majesty will be wearing the uniform of either the Grenadier Guards, the Scots, the Welsh or the Irish Guards, the Coldstream Guards, the Royal Horse Guards or the Life Guards.

On arrival, she mounts a white horse and, with an escort of one selected officer, proceeds to inspect the massed troops and to take the salute; as she does this, the massed bands of the regiments concerned play martial music. Only one Colour is 'trooped' on each of these ceremonial occasions: that of each regiment in strict rotation. Having taken the salute, the monarch returns with her escort to Buckingham Palace at the head of her Guards, whose duty it is, again in strict rotation, to mount guard at the palace so long as she is in residence there and not away at Windsor, Balmoral, Sandringham, or abroad.

Ce déploiement de faste militaire, institué par George II, a lieu le deuxième samedi de Juin. Sa Majesté la Reine revêt l'uniforme d'un des régiments dont elle est Colonel-en-Chef. Sur son cheval blanc, elle inspecte les troupes; un drapeau est présenté, celui de chaque régiment à tour de rôle.

Jedes Jahr zum offiziellen Geburtstag des regierenden Monarchen findet diese glänzende Zeremonie statt. Nur eine Fahne von den verschiedenen Regimenten wird jedes Jahr abgenommen.

EDINBURGH: MILITARY TATTOO

This is the most spectacular and generally popular feature of the annual Edinburgh International Festival of Music and Drama, now a quarter-century old. It is held on the terrace of Edinburgh Castle which, from its rocky bluff, dominates the city. It is a colourful spectacle both of sight and of sound, for the massed formation movements and the intricate dancing by the men of the Highland Brigade and other units with historic traditions are performed to that unique sound that stirs the hearts of all but the stone-deaf: the skirl of the bagpipes.

There are numerous other examples of the degree to which men can be trained to perform military exercises, with or without the accompaniment of the music of military bands; but there is nothing quite comparable with what may be seen at this ceremony, so essentially Scottish in tradition and in spirit. Most notable is the period during which the massed bands of the various regiments parade across the arena, marching and playing with absolute precision and immense power. Floodlighting adds a dramatic element to the entertainment. Though fundamentally a Scottish occasion, in the past ten years or so additional colour has been provided, often of an exotic character, by the marching and dancing of soldiers from, for example, some of the South Pacific islands. But it is ever the bagpipes that dominate!

Ce divertissement son et lumière, est le trait le plus populaire du Festival annuel de Musique et de Théâtre, et a lieu sur la terrasse du Château. C'est un spectacle à la fois pour l'oeil et pour l'oreille, comprenant des danses, des exercices militaires et beaucoup de musique.

Der Zapfenstreich gehört zu den populärsten Darbietungen des Edinbugh International Festival of Drama and Music und findet auf der Terrasse des Edinburgh Castle statt, wobei das Tanzen der Highland Brigade ein farbenfreudiges Schauspiel bietet.

LONDON: LORD MAYOR'S SHOW

This most spectacular and popular annual event takes place on the Saturday nearest to 9 November. The newly elected Lord Mayor rides in a gilded coach drawn by six Shire horses. He is accompanied by the City Marshal and escorted by liveried retainers and his own bodyguard, the Company of Pikemen and Musketeers drawn from the Honourable Artillery Company though they wear historic uniforms and weaponry as a reminder that the ceremony dates back seven centuries to the reign of King John, who decreed that London's Lord Mayor must present himself publicly to its citizens.

His protracted journey commences at the Mansion House and is carefully timed so that he arrives at the Royal Courts of Justice exactly at noon. Here he swears before the Lord Chief Justice and the Bench that he will faithfully perform those duties that devolve upon him during his term of office. He then formally invites the Justices to dine with him later on at Guildhall, and departs for the Mansion House, the Lord Mayor's official residence for two centuries past. His 'comet's-tail' procession becomes more elaborate every year. Often a mile in length, it consists largely of a train of ornamental tableaux-on-wheels ingeniously devised to portray some specific theme with which he may personally be involved.

L'évènement le plus spectaculaire et populaire a lieu le samedi le plus proche du 9 novembre. Le Lord Mayor nouvellement élu doit se présenter à ses citoyens. Suivi d'un cortège de plus en plus raffiné, il se rend en carrosse doré, tiré par six chevaux, aux "Royal Courts of Justice", où il doit prêter serment.

Dieses farbenfreudige und beliebte Ereignis findet nach der Wahl des Oberbürgermeisters von London statt. Dieser fährt in einer Goldkutsche, gezogen von sechs Pferden, durch die City und seine Eskorte besteht aud Leibwächtern, Musketieren und einer Ehrenkavallerie. Ihm folgt ein oft Kilometer langer Umzug.

WALES: PROCLAIMING THE BARD AT THE ROYAL NATIONAL EISTEDDFOD

Unlike the International Music Eisteddfod, held annually at Llangollen, this is essentially an all-Welsh institution, the relatively modern version of a bardic festival that dates back at least twelve centuries. The Welsh word is a contraction of the full title: 'Session of the Bards of the Island of Britain' and, as this implies, is a festival of Welsh-only Drama, Literature, Verse-speaking and Music, including the unique Penillion Singing. It is officially 'proclaimed' a year-and-a-day in advance, and dominated by the Arch Druid, who wears over his robes a copper breastplate and is crowned with a coronet of oak leaves.

The ceremony, always in the first week of August and held alternately in north and south Wales, is conducted throughout in Welsh. He raises aloft the Sword of Peace and cries out: 'Is It Peace?'. The response, 'Heddwch!' (Peace It Is!) reverberates from a thousand throats. The culmination of the competitions in singing, dramatic presentation and verse-speaking is the festival's 'Chair Day', when the composer of the winning poem – in a highly stylised form and metre – is announced; he takes his place in the coveted Bardic Chair to receive the even more coveted Bardic Crown. As the crown is bestowed upon him he receives also an appropriate Bardic Name, which he proudly bears from that moment onwards.

Cette institution est une version moderne du festival de Poésie Celtique, datant de 12 siècles. Cette cérémonie est célébrée en gallois, au nord ou au sud du Pays de Galles, en août, et présidée par un Druide coiffé d'une couronne en feuilles de chêne.

Dies walisische Festspiel ist eine moderne Version bardischer Tradition, die über zwölf Jahrhunderte zurückgeht und ist der walisischen Dichtung, dem Theater, der Literatur und der Musik gewidmet. Der Dichter, der den ersten Preis erhält, wird traditionell gekrönt und enthält einen bardischen Namen.

WINDSOR: THE GARTER CEREMONY

The highest Order in British Chivalry is the Most Noble Order of the Garter, founded by Edward III in 1348; its motto is *Honi Soit Qui Mal Y Pense*. Companionship of the Order is strictly limited to the monarch, members of the Royal Family, and 25 Knights, the Military Knights of Windsor; also some overseas members. Uniquely, it possesses its own chapel – St George's, Windsor Castle.

The Investiture of a new Knight, a brilliant occasion, takes place in the Throne Room. The monarch, wearing the Sovereign's Mantle of the Order, buckles the Garter on his left leg, places the mantle and collar on his shoulders, and presents him with the Star of the Order and the Ribbon, worn transversely across the chest. After this, the newly created Knight takes the solemn oath. Then the Pursuivants, Heralds, Kings-of-Arms and Military Knights process between two ranks of dismounted Household Cavalrymen to the Chapel of St George for the Garter Service. Particularly impressive are the 12 Military Knights of the Order, men who are permanently in residence in Windsor Castle itself. They wear brilliantly variegated uniforms consisting of scarlet tailcoats, broad-striped blue trousers and black silk cocked hats adorned with red and white flowing plumes.

L'Ordre le plus élevé de la Chevalerie britannique est l'Ordre de la Jarretière, dont la devise est "Honi soit qui mal y pense". L'investiture d'un nouveau chevalier est une cérémonie éclatante, qui a lieu dans la Salle du Trône à Windsor, suivie d'un office à la Chapelle St Georges.

Der höchste britische Ritterorden ist der Hosenbandorden, der unter dem Motto 'Honi Soit Qui Mal T Pense' von Eduard III. im Jahre 1348 gegründet wurde. Der Orden besteht nur aus Mitgliedern der königlichen Familie und einer geringen Zahl von Rittern; er hat seine eigene Kirche im Schloss Windsor.